NINE SERI

Mischief Of One Kind And Another

Jennie E. Owen
Jen Feroze
Ben Tufnell

Published by Nine Pens

2024

www.ninepens.co.uk

ISBN: 978-1-917150-00-2

NS 009

Jennie E. Owen

Jennie E. Owen has been published in a large range of journals and anthologies including the *Rialto, Wasafiri, Agenda Poetry, Acumen, Neon, Envoi, Tears in the Fence, Iota,* and *Magma Poetry*. She is Best of the Net, Pushcart and Forward Prize nominated. Jennie's pamphlet 'The Horses Still Run' will be published by The Flight of the Dragonfly Press later in 2024.

Jennie teaches Creative Writing for The Open University and lives in Lancashire, UK with her husband and three children. She is a PhD student at Manchester Metropolitan University, focusing on poetry and place.

The Crying Boy
Giovanni Bragolin (1911-1981)

He doesn't look the sort to start a fire
to scorch your house, too young, too weary
to play with matches; all the heat
sits in his fevered cheek. So remember,
you were the ones that called for the burning:
piling child, frame and drift wood. You
should have known that such distress is not
displayed in a front room, like an antique trinket
porcelain dog or silver backed heirloom. He does not belong
in the hall way, or kitchenette. This lost shadow
before shadow, wet and dark-eyed, the hint
of a trembling lip.
$\qquad\qquad\qquad$ Sooty toddler, he could be yours,
this sticky fingered infant of war.
$\qquad\qquad\qquad$ Yet you all
proclaimed him the monster, built the bonfire.
So only now he creeps
$\qquad\qquad\qquad$ the edge
$\qquad\qquad\qquad\qquad$ like a flame,
$\qquad\qquad\qquad\qquad$ (like a threat)

Sedlec Ossuary
Cemetery Church of All Saints, Prague (built around 1400)

I did not believe it was you even then, not until
I saw the shape of your face beneath the shroud;
an invisible expression, grist and mill,

derision I'd witnessed a thousand times before.
There were the blades, slicing a dish. I looked away,
as they counted your ribs down, one by one. I'd

once kissed that chest, those collar bones; owl pellets
filled with the needles and pins of voles and mice.
Your hands are saintly relics, I wish now

I could steal a chip of metacarpal to place
inside a velvet box, to ward off the ache you'd cause
one day, I held the weight of your head in my lap,

a chandelier of ivory, where a bare cathedral
of teeth met with concentric circles of yellow
marrow. Your spine was always twitching roadkill.

Your heart, when they tear it open, will release
a murder of crows, to circle and beat the air.

The Anguished Man and the Rain Woman go on a date
(Unknown artist)   *(Svetlana Telets 1996)*

He keeps her waiting outside the bar.

It's raining loose change, bouncing off the tarmac in shivers
that slide down her neck, into her bra.

She's less annoyed than she supposes when he arrives,
wiping his face
along his sleeve (something so boyish in that one action)

She's always been attracted to red heads, her own complexion
so pale her eyes are bruises beneath her black hat, black scarf.

Halfway into the starter she knows they will not meet again.

She sips at her iced water deeply, watches him eat ravening,
wolfish.
His mouth is open, breath full of chilli, flecks of orange

between his teeth. She pushes around her pearls of fish
as he vibrates the air with short talk and long stories. She
learns

that they never end well. The blood rises in his cheeks,
he stabs the air for emphasis. She picks her plate silver and
thin,

dainty as his knife. She's been told, her silence intimidates,
like falling into to a lake, one lover said. She absorbs.

She drowns. He takes a moment, a breath, asks her
if she'd like a dessert, a cocktail? *Sorry she says*

I have an early start. But even in that moment

she sees herself stood outside under the rain,
letting it wash through her clothes till they

cling to her skin. Stood in the downpour until
at dawn it softens to a drizzle.

Man Proposes, God Disposes
Edwin Landseer 1864

This is the land of seracs, of cold mist
spectres that rise like sheer drops, of crushing
wood and ice, thin air freezing every breath
in the exhale. We could be the horrors
but are not, are no match for this hunger,
this blue grey force, the bare and pin-picked corpse.
This is trespass, you the only witness
of broken angles, the red twisted mast
lurching forward, it ruptures the surface.
You can feel the teeth at your sleeves, and then
the breath at your throat. We all become dark
fossils, under pressure of endeavour.
You know the truth now, there's no way home.
Each monster devours you; spit, blood and bone

The Silver Basano Vase

15th Century. Maker unknown.
Location unknown.

The clutch and size of a heart,
this sleeping bride, holds
it to her chest, she, who will never
live to press an infant there.

It remains egg warm in her hands,
despite the chill night,
despite the goose flesh
that had come, and long since
passed. She wields the silver
vessel that is stained with cruor;
as though she had plucked
the thing from the teeth
of her ribs, ripped
it out by the half-moons
of her fingertips.

This bride is emptied out,
so hollow, a single tap
will ring out like the mourning
of small birds (who go on to catch
the dawn streak in their beaks)

To you, this story exists
only in time, so the shape
is familiar in your mouth. You
pass it on as a kiss, heated breath
in the ear. But much of it
has been hidden away,

buried underground,
sealed in a leaden box with a dozen
gothic curiosities; a pale cord
of girls heads hanging
behind a locked door.

Blood can be washed
from a gimcrack such as this,
soon forgotten
with elbow grease,
with soap and water. The foxing
of her touch buffed out. But

she once held it to her chest,
the weight:
of a wedding breakfast,
of a bridal wreath.

This simple action now
works in reverse, the curse
is a backward step,
the face of a clock
in the mirror. She sees herself
placing the vase onto the shelf
on a clear cold night. Her
lover
arriving early, will lead her
away from this place,
this very moment.

When she will at last be filled
to her brim,
to overflowing.

The Hands Resist Him
Bill Stoneham (1972)

We bought the painting from e-bay, we thought it was a fake,
a talking point we could hang in the hallway (it gets dark
quickly there)
He assumed both figures were haunted dolls, no I tell him, the
boy is the artist.
We bought the painting from e-bay, we thought it was a fake
bet it takes forever cleaning that window, he says, all those
fingerprints.
We bought the painting from e-bay, we wish it was a fake
a talking point we could hang in the hallway (it gets dark
quickly there)

Oliver Cromwell's Death Mask
Thomas Simon (1658) National Portrait Gallery

The skin should still be warm,
caught before it sinks or swells, to ensure
a likeness. Wrap a sheet around the neck.
Grease the face well. Check that you push
into the sockets, the lines at the mouth. Slide
further than the hairline and past
the ears. Eyes should be fully closed,
the facial hair groomed.
Plaster and bandages
come next. It takes skill
to ensure that first layer captures the mien
of innocent rest, no matter who. Take patience here
to smooth every last air bubble. Further layers
will build on the integrity
capture a broken nose, a distinguished mole.
Wait an hour.
Carefully peel   away
the impression. Remove
any residue, (professionals
leave no trace)
Wax can be purchased easily enough
to melt over the stove,
to pour with a steady hand.
My customers
always report their satisfaction
(for it is a craft) One widow
sleeps with her husband's likeness on his pillow.
I have even served royalty, or almost.
for it is said Cromwell's likeness
wore the crown.

The Dead Mother and Child
Edvard Munch (1863 – 1944)

I know I am a painting, that much I understand.
I'm rendered in flat blocks of red and orange. A small girl
floating in front of black impressions, blank faces.

They drift backwards, slide away and I push my hands
over my ears. I want to close my eyes, but instead
I watch you walking to and fro in the gallery

I count each easy footstep and ignore the others
who share my plane. I know they exist only to push me
forward through the thick layers of linseed and turps.

There is a connection between me and the corpse
but in this moment I cannot place what it is. She lies,
not peacefully. Not at peace. But there she lies, ironed out
flat.

I cannot remember who my creator is.
(The name is signed too thickly in the corner to see)

But then I do.

The Fall of the Rebel Angels
Master of the Rebel Angels (painted between 1340 and 1345)

All auric fire and red
this holy glitter globe war,
of beautiful monsters
paper cut shades.

Shake it up, watch them fall
observe them as they scold the Earth
as we catch them with
open arms aflame.

But upend the image,
they soar away.

Jen Feroze

Jen Feroze lives by the sea in Essex with her husband and two young children. A former Foyle Young Poet, her work has appeared in publications including *Under the Radar, Butcher's Dog, Magma, Poetry Wales, Spelt, One Hand Clapping* and *The Alchemy Spoon*. She has guest edited anthologies for Black Bough Poetry and The Mum Poem Press, and she placed second in the 2022/2023 Magma Editors' Prize. Her debut pamphlet 'Tiny Bright Thorns' is publishing in 2024 with Nine Pens. Jen loves cold water swimming, chunky knitwear, amaretto sours and cheese you can eat with a spoon. Find her on the artist formerly known as Twitter @jenlareine and on Instagram @the_colourofhope.

A Duplex For Rumpelstiltskin

After The Brothers Grimm

He should have known better,
the jewels came so easily from her neck.

So easily, or so he thought. Simple jewels, barely shining
but set in gold, coaxed into his clawed hands.

She watched his twisted hands coaxing gold from straw,
hay-scent becoming riches recognised by men, by kings.

She was straw-scented as king's riches swelled within her
and she remembered everything she'd ever heard.

Everything she'd ever heard whispered in the woods noted,
logged like the sacks of flour in the old barn.

She is heavy as a sack of flour, dulled and heavy, he thinks.
Slowly she lulled him as he spun.

Now she is a mother, spinning slowly among her baby's
playthings.
She knows all their names. He should have known better.

On Missel Moor

After Frances Hodgson Burnett

When she said 'nobody wants me' and
'why is it always so cold here?', and
'I have spoken, all depart!'
I wanted to take her dancing in predawn fog.
Wanted to watch her downturned mouth for hours
for signs of spring, paint her sour-milk cheeks
with moorland rain and heather
and wait for them to bloom red.

I wanted to gift her sycamore keys
for her many locked doors, shock her
with the snap of a winter twig –
seemingly brittle as her unloved bones –
to show her the way it is shot through with green
at the marrow.

Irreconcilable Differences
After Edward Lear

Looking back now, at the way
this whole mess was immortalised,
the first thing I take issue with is the colour.

An easy rhythm for a man
who has never seen a pea,
who has never spent a night on a rough sea,

who has never felt
fur and feathers saltclumped,
this sudden unwelcome weight.

That boat was the colour of regret, that's all.
The colour of haste.
We 'went to sea' – how easy it is to say.

Ignore the clamour of angry voices,
the teeth at our heels.
The honey lay thick on our tongues.

When there was finally a moon
to steer by, it looked hollow.
I remember standing on the edge

of the sand with the trees tolling behind us.
I remember the strangeness of wattle and squawk,
the cold eyes of the forest hogs.

When I think of him now, it's talon and spite.
But I remember him singing, yes.
That much, at least, is true.

Catching A Tiger
After Judith Kerr

Sophie's mummy was different afterwards;
her gaze flicking towards the door.

Tea parties every day, always the same,
the table arranged just so – buns, biscuits, sandwiches,

the brown pot for tea,
even when the handle cracked.

And she never bought just one set of groceries,
instead she filled the cupboards and the pantry

until they avalanched with packets and tins.
Sauces and boxes and cereals and jams.

pans bubbling over on the stove.
The fridge was filled with steak and sausage,

venison and pheasant in game season. Sophie's mummy
had made fast friends with the butcher.

Sophie found she couldn't enter a room
without finding a plate of meat on the sill,

the window thrown wide and beckoning.
Sophie's Daddy spent more time at work,

he ate his dinners at the café.
Sophie sometimes dreamed of teeth and fur.

She heard a shiver of deep purr through a closed door;
noticed her mummy's eyes flashing amber over breakfast.

Moving Day
After The Brothers Grimm

For weeks now, the house has been haunted
by the suits and shoes of zealous estate agents.
The dark hush of the trees – excellent allies,
excellent secret-keepers – was felled
a long time ago in the name of the city's loud expansion.
Now there is nowhere to hide.

Hard candy smiles pass through each room, looking out
through sugar-glass panes they convince themselves are dusky
and bubbled with age alone; running their hands
over mantels and recoiling at the layer of dust
on their fingertips. The house holds its breath,
waiting for someone to touch their lips, to taste its sweetness.

Then this afternoon, a truck yellow as sherbet lemons arrived
and spilled four bright, warm lives out and inside. So much noise
and so many running feet after so much gnawing emptiness,
so much guilt. The boxes smell hopeful. They make the house
ache.
There are two children – a boy and a girl,
curls soft as candyfloss.

They delight in choosing their new bedroom;
they fall asleep without a story, without a nightlight.
Downstairs, their parents clink glasses of cheap wine
as night arrives at the windows. They discuss where to hang
the family photographs, who they should call
to look at the old oven that didn't want to light this evening.

If the house could talk, it would tell them to buy a new one,
shamed by the wicked pile of ash that still covers the grill.

If the house could talk, it would press upon them the wisdom of keeping breadcrumbs close at hand, even in the absence of trees.

It would feel a slow tide of sugar rising unstoppably in its walls at the sound of laughter, at the thought of those little, darting tongues.

The Railway Children
After E. Nesbitt

When I was ten, I wanted their house.
The rolling hills, their mother
and buns for tea, the rough friendship
of Mr Perks; even their sadness
that I didn't understand.
But most of all I wanted their trains.

I still get that swooping feeling
in my stomach whenever it roars past
like a great dragon – the three of them
perched on that wooden fence –
and every window is open,
blocked by smiling faces,
by waving, white handkerchiefs.

Neverland Kisses
After J M Barrie

These days I drop my kisses
like a gull. Swoop, dive and away
frequently eye-rolled, cheek-rubbed.

'She's growing up' –
refrained like rainfall
from knowing elders.

I disagree; look to your beach pebbles,
the fistfuls of leaves stuffed
clumsy in school dress pockets.

The magpie feather left stark
on the pavement.
Your indignant rage.

These are your thimbles
your acorn buttons.
Just let me watch

as you lift your small chin
to the sky, and head straight on
'til morning.

Climate Change
After C.S Lewis

The citizens of Cair Paravel
roll the word around their mouths –
winter; certain it was something
they used to be able to bite down on.

Rivers are treacherous now.
A constant creak of thaw and freeze,
impossible to cross. There have been drownings.
The beavers have long since moved on.

The stone table is fatigued with heat,
latticed with cracks long before
it is lionised; before it has to bear
the grief of the land.

In the wood, the green is brittle, tired;
sap tang hangs thick in the air.
The lamp post shines defiant against the sun,
metal angry enough to burn.

Snow here is talcum powder fine,
barely enough to leave a boot mark.
Jadis whips the white deer harder –
dusty blood and sweat in rivulets.

She shrugs off her furs.
Looks to the white-hot sky.

Mischief of One Kind and Another
After Maurice Sendak

The trees were first to spot him. Gossipy. They said 'wild'.
We didn't pay them much mind, after all, we were bred wild.

He was wolf pelted, baby faced, a paper-crowned captain
smelling of soap, love – a warm gingerbread wild.

We were old, tired, claws sheathed, sleep ready. Strange
that this slender child made us rumpus instead, wild!

He danced us hypnotic, led us jungle deep, moon drunk;
hooting and laughing, turned our calls and our tread wild.

We'd forgotten this freedom, the flow of night in our blood.
He awoke something in us we'd kept long unfed. Wild

and thrumming, we loved him. We lifted him high
'til he turned on his wolf's heels and suddenly fled wild

we chased him offshore, talons raking sea foam
still he sailed off and left us there, back to his bedwild.

Some of us stand, howling 'Max' to the dark sea,
in and out of weeks, our throats keening red, wild.

Ben Tufnell

Ben Tufnell is a curator and writer based in London. His poems have been published by *Anthropocene, Entropy, Pangyrus, The Rialto, Shearsman* and *Smartish Pace*, amongst others, and his stories have been published by *Conjunctions, Litro*, Nightjar Press, *Storgy* and *Structo*. He has been longlisted for the BBC Short Story Award and shortlisted for the Society of Authors' ALCS Tom-Gallon Trust Award. His debut novel 'The North Shore' is published by Fleet (Little, Brown).

Memento

Houses are not haunted
but people are. We carry

our ghosts within, oblique
resonances, doubtful glimpses.

My house is not empty and
my head is an echo chamber.

Outside, the garden is a skeleton,
the sky the whiter part of the eye.

I stained it with some words
like 'winter' and 'ash'

and the hush isn't really silence, being
broken by the drone of combustion,

the barking of dogs, the sounding
of sirens, passing trains, pounding,

faint sighs, the wash of wind through
the bare bark of dead black trees

and the rumble of blood in your ears:
the churning of thoughts, urgent fears.

It is the sound of all our fine constructions
being ground to dust and dirt

as the knotweed forces its way up
through the oil-spotted earth

and the tangled creeper
at the bottom of the path

bursts spectacularly into
wildly perfumed flower.

The Eroding Shore

The shadows, remote -
the fugitive memories,
remainings and echoes
of vague histories -

are as quick and contingent
as the fox or the hawk, even
the hare, those wild and
unruly shades, fleeting,

just seen, little more
than a shadow, a tint,
a flicker of presence
breaking the edge

of the field of vision,
or crossing the lane
where the willows sway,
above the reeded stream

which quietly winds
a slow silvery thread
through darkness
to the sea.

The sea, just a few miles
from here, as the crow flies,
which, hypnotic, pulls
at the land, stone by stone.

From the shingle banks
which yield slowly,
thirty years ago, alone,
I flew a kite.

It seems to me
it still hangs there.

Owls

We lived in a house of owls,
their planetary eyes tracking
my childhood years; sentinels,
strangely silent, always still.

One in particular, the long-eared
eagle - *Bubo bubo* - haunted
my sleep. He watched me, patient.
His unblinking eyes: Jupiter and Mars.

Now, by night, in a garden,
the cry that comes unexpected
through the city, resonant,
the soft bass exhalation – *ooh hu* –

is a portal, a calling, and I am
instantly deep in the dream-forest
of the past, tracing journeys
on mist breath and moon wing,

hunting through trees in ecstatic
silence, flying low along the old lane
towards the sea and then out into
openness; intent, ethereal, apex.

Crocodile

The childhood dream
of the gnarled beast beneath
the bed. Long rotting grin
slowly opening and closing
with a castanet click
in thick darkness.
Waiting, still.

My father would have to kneel down
and reach in and make great play,
a dumb show in the shadows,
of pulling him out and
wrestling him to the top of the stairs
and then throwing him down.
It was a nightly ritual.

But I knew, even then, that
he would always climb back up,
his pale scaly belly scraping
the bare edges of each stair
and then silently across carpet
to creep back under the bed
to wait once more.

Yellow peg teeth in darkness,
stoned eye, like a stone, in darkness,
the weight of him, in darkness,
black carved claws in darkness,
saw-edged tail heavy in darkness,
a spell, occult, in darkness,
stilled, apprehensive, in darkness.

To wait once more
for the unsleeping child
to drift or forget, and let
limp foot or finger
fall from between sheets,
and linger within reach.
Waiting, still.

And now, even now,
when the night is unquiet
and sleep is a shadow
I slip into and out of,
I hear the slow slither,
the click-clacking teeth,
and know he climbs up still
for me, and always will.

Ghosts

Something becomes visible
against the windows of the house

like condensation or the delicate web
of cold on winter mornings,

the frosting of breath - of words
arriving, thoughts becoming,

the tiny crystals of reason
knitted surely into a fine veil -

and the garden, and everything,
slips behind this fragile film

of mist, transcendent,
as darkness gains in weight

and at such moments
we are frail, impermanent.

Exhaust

It seemed that the world might burst open
like a heart pumped too full of blood.

We put our backs against the damp ground
and our souls fluttered up into the sky,

things of gossamer, threads of silver
faint sounds, a depression in the fabric of air.

It's true, I heard the flapping of wings
above us in the cracked tree fingers

and something blew through me and shook me
that wasn't the wind, but was silvery,

and at such times it might seem
that this is what we add up to:

a wish or a glimpse,
a fleeting image, the condensation of thought

and the hollowness of cold that fills
you up and leaves you breathless and blind

when things won't hold together, but slip
and rub against each other and cancel each the other out,

awash in the day, ragged in the night
and crushed in the grey area in between.

The Ice Age

In the cupboard
the continents shift
and glaciers knock
as snow forms drifts,
and time is compressed.

Beneath the bed
unsmiling cracks open in ice
revealing stony ground
and all is stilled by an
advancing white shadow.

The wardrobe holds
the memories of a life
but all that has been ground
down to dust, milled fine
to a subtle tilth.

The fireplace is a cold dark
mouth, an empty grave. Snow
is piled deep like pillows
and now is the time to sleep
as the grey ice creeps,

tectonically slow, pushing
aside the furniture and grinding
the mirror to glittering sand.

Dust

Just days after placing the book
on the shelf I run a finger

across the cover and leave a
wake of shadow.

In a dictionary I read
this example of usage:

'The dictionaries
were covered in *dust*.'

So here are the disintegrating
pages, something worthless,

very small particles of earth
or sand. A fine powder which

consists of very small particles
of a substance such as gold,

wood or coal. A fine dry
powder consisting of earth

or waste matter
lying on the ground

or on surfaces or
carried in the air.

Fine particles of matter
(as of earth). Spilth.

The particles into which
something disintegrates.

Dirt, sand, flakes or filth.
Soot, ashes, fragments, wax.

Something worthless. Dried
earth reduced to powder.

A cloud of finely powdered earth
or other matter in the air.

The surface of the ground.
A fine dry powder. Chaff.

Stars, pale fires, a cosmos.
Countless constellations.

This too: the earth, as the resting place
of the dead. The earthly remains

of bodies once alive; the remains
of the human body. Debris.

Entropic vapour. Remainings.
Something worthless.

On the shelves the books are
slowly and softly buried

beneath the drifting matter:
the shadow of life.

The Moon Shifts

The stopcock creaks and drips
as deep inside the walls
old pipes groan and shudder.

The clock stops. A thick
sheet shrouds the head.
The menagerie beneath the bed

hold their breath and wait
in anticipation of the stray finger,
the unprotected toe.

And if I do not breathe
I can hear the spiders spinning
and the dust motes drifting,

even the soft exhalation
of a shooting star expiring
somewhere in the stratosphere

in that distant liminal zone,
outer, in between, neither
of this world or another.

These soft songs echo about
the empty chambers of the inner
ear; induce tiny bones to shudder.

The night brain clicks and whirrs
like a clock mechanism, a precision
instrument without precise purpose,

keeping a kind of time: vague hours,
infinite seconds. The night brain thumps
and booms as hot blood races through

the soft matter nestled in its stony pocket.
Dull nerves. Restless fingers. The evening
shiver. The midnight twitch.

We revolve slowly beneath
the speckled heavens, spinning
through space, one eye on the eye

of the moon, distant, glimpsed
through a thin gap in the drape,
a sickled silver slit.

She waits up by the ceiling
where the darkness is darker,
where the spiders spin.

She watches the flickering films
precarious behind the screen of my eyelids,
closed, suffused with blood.

I wait here, watching through closed eyes.
She drifts with the dust and the ghosts,
carried on air currents so delicate

they do not even stir the fine hairs
on the back of my hands. The clock ticks.
The moon shifts. The stopcock clicks.

Acknowledgements

Jen

Many thanks to the editors of: *Under the Radar*, where Irreconcilable Differences was first published *iamb*, where Moving Day was first published

Ben

Thanks to the editors of the following publications in which these poems first appeared: 'The Eroding Shore' and 'Ghosts' in *La Picioletta Barca,* 'Owls' in *Entropy*, 'Crocodile' in *San Antonio Review,* and 'Exhaust' in *Pangyrus.*